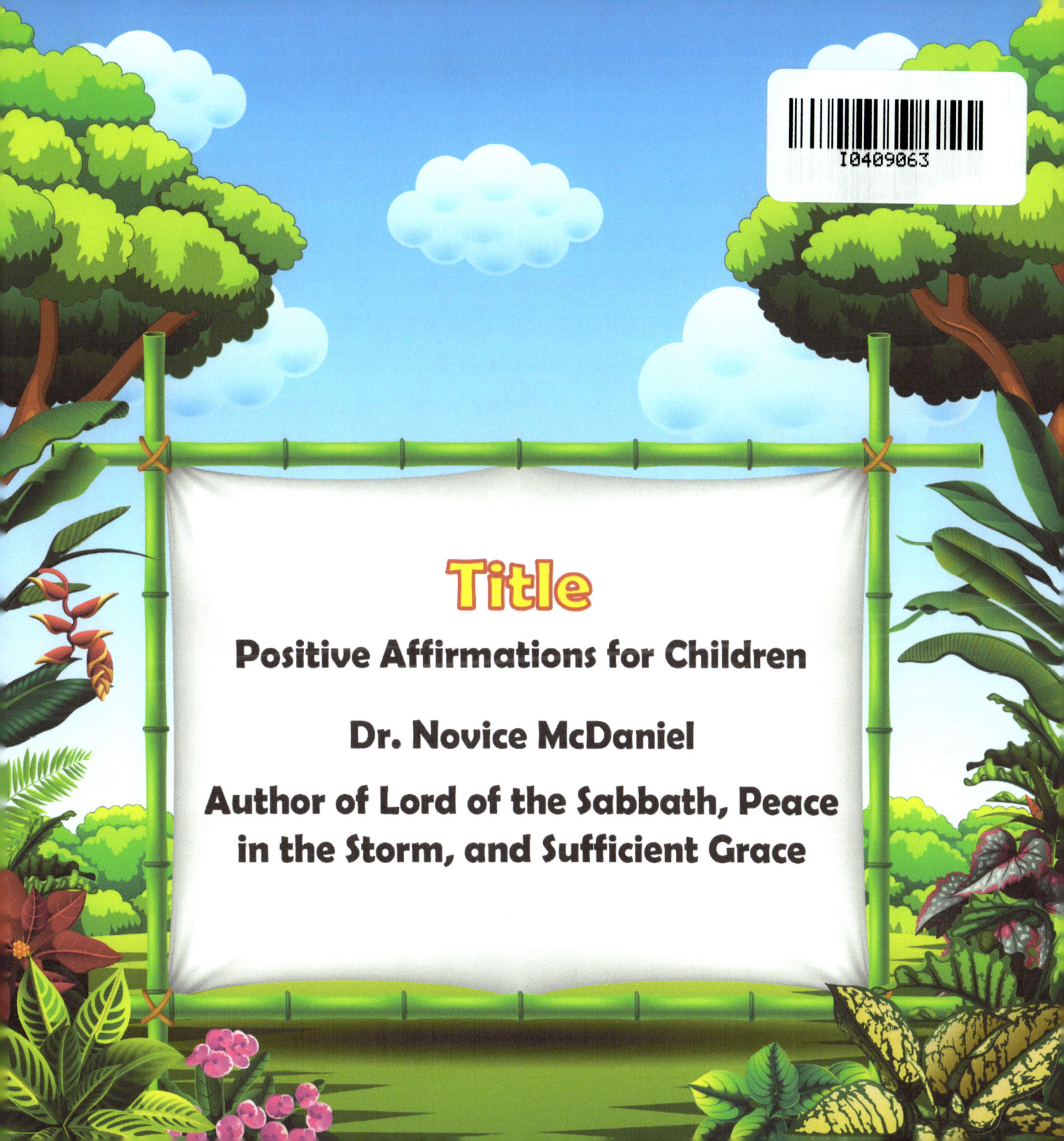

# Title

**Positive Affirmations for Children**

**Dr. Novice McDaniel**

**Author of Lord of the Sabbath, Peace in the Storm, and Sufficient Grace**

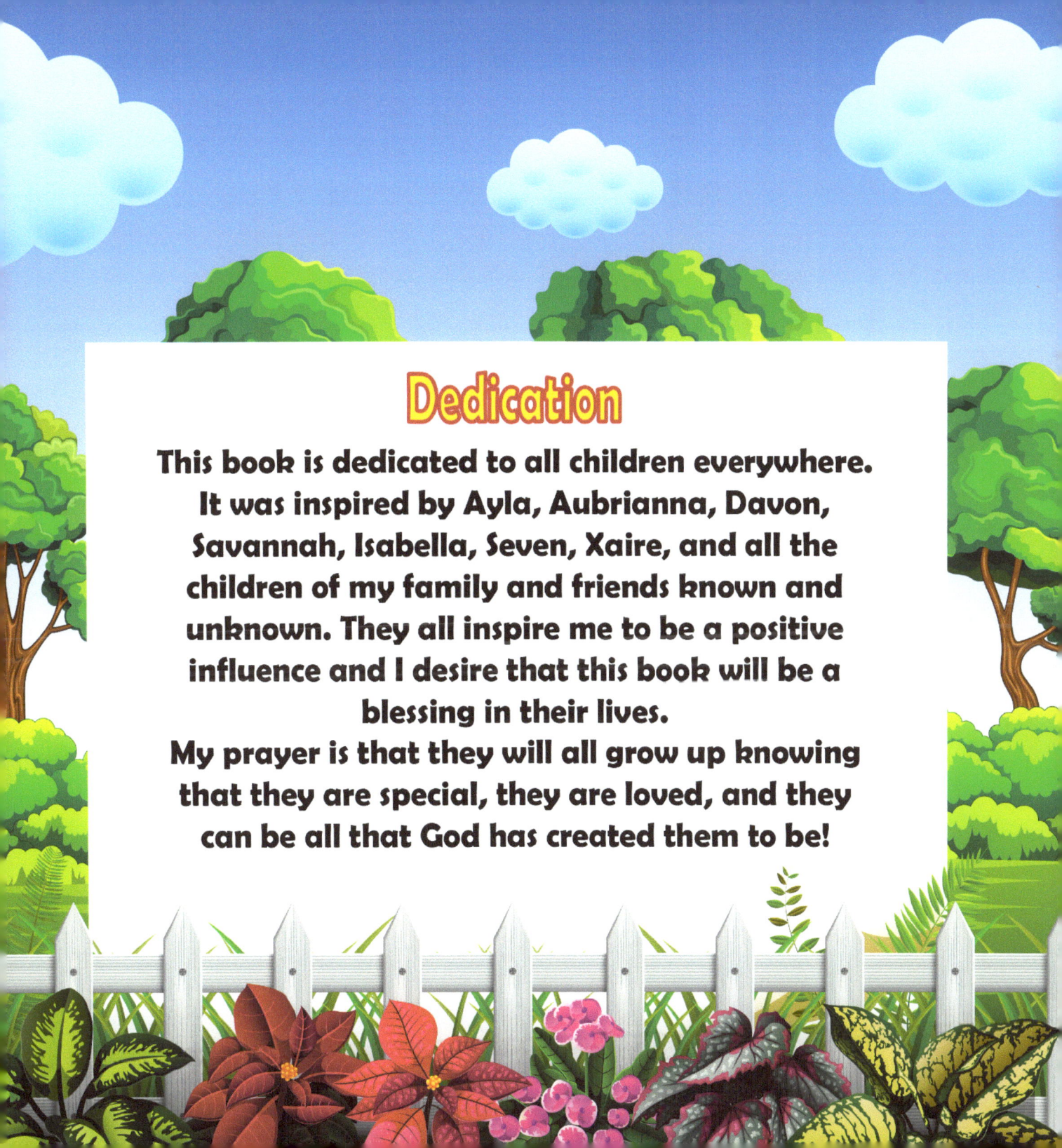

# Dedication

This book is dedicated to all children everywhere. It was inspired by Ayla, Aubrianna, Davon, Savannah, Isabella, Seven, Xaire, and all the children of my family and friends known and unknown. They all inspire me to be a positive influence and I desire that this book will be a blessing in their lives.

My prayer is that they will all grow up knowing that they are special, they are loved, and they can be all that God has created them to be!

# Introduction

Introducing, "Positive Affirmations for Children"- a delightful and empowering book filled with uplifting messages to inspire young minds. Each page is brimming with colorful illustrations and cheerful affirmations that encourage children to believe in themselves, embrace their uniqueness, and cultivate positive mindsets. With heartfelt words and captivating imagery, this book aims to nurture self-confidence, foster resilience, and promote a healthy sense of self-worth in children. "Positive Affirmations for Children" is a treasure trove of positivity that will illuminate the hearts of young readers, guiding them towards a bright and promising future.

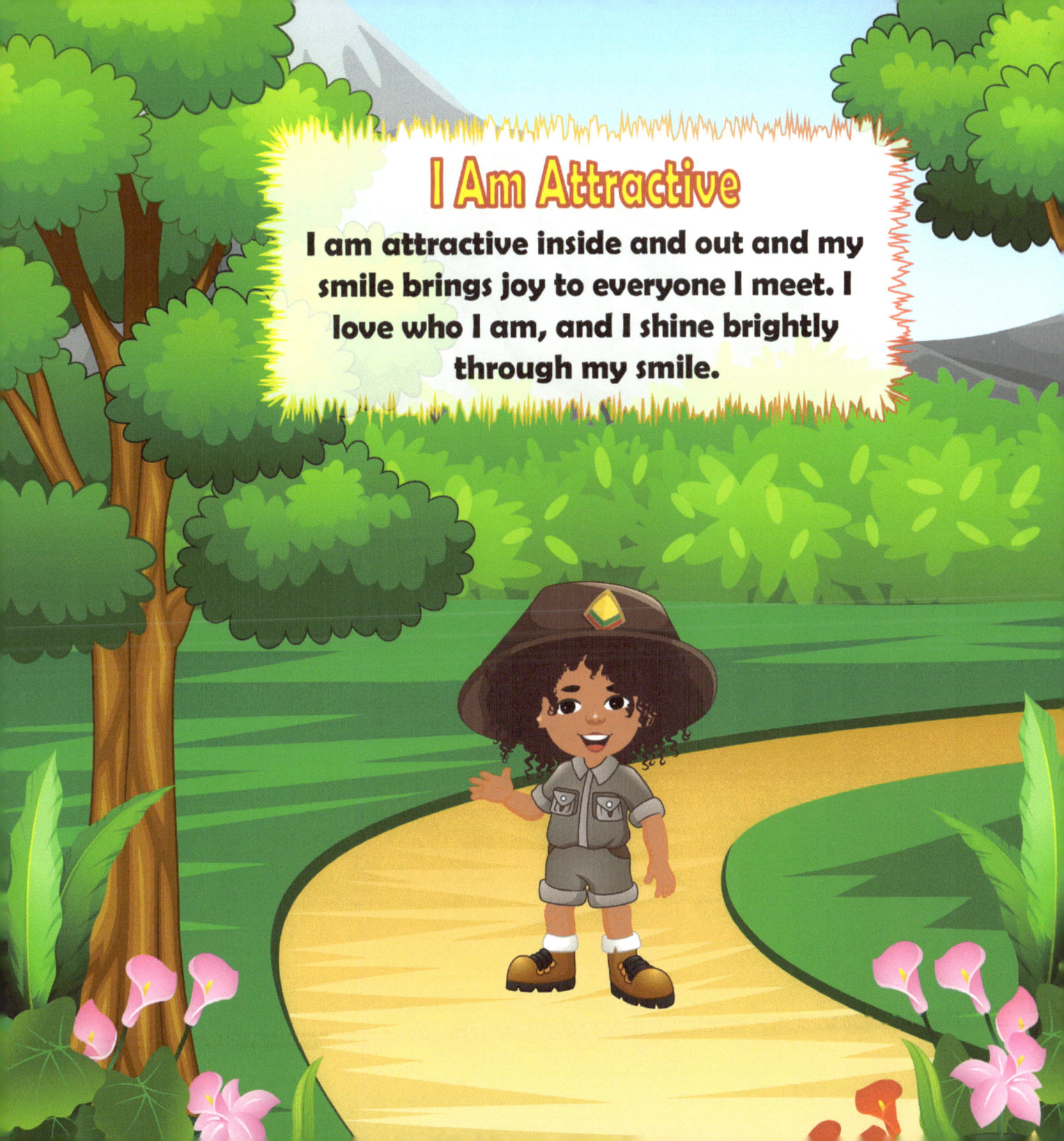

# I Am Attractive

I am attractive inside and out and my smile brings joy to everyone I meet. I love who I am, and I shine brightly through my smile.

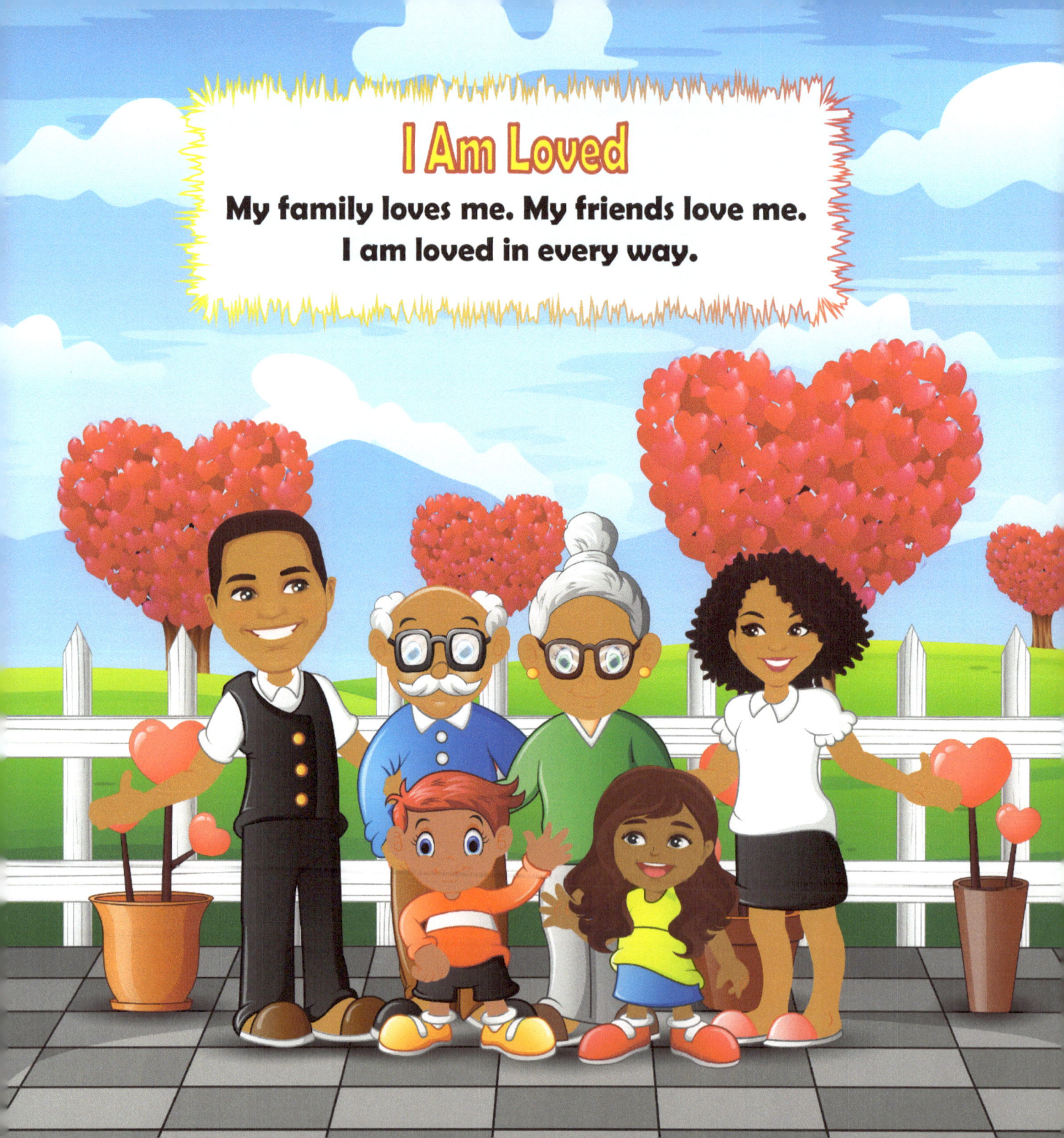

# I Am Loved

My family loves me. My friends love me.
I am loved in every way.

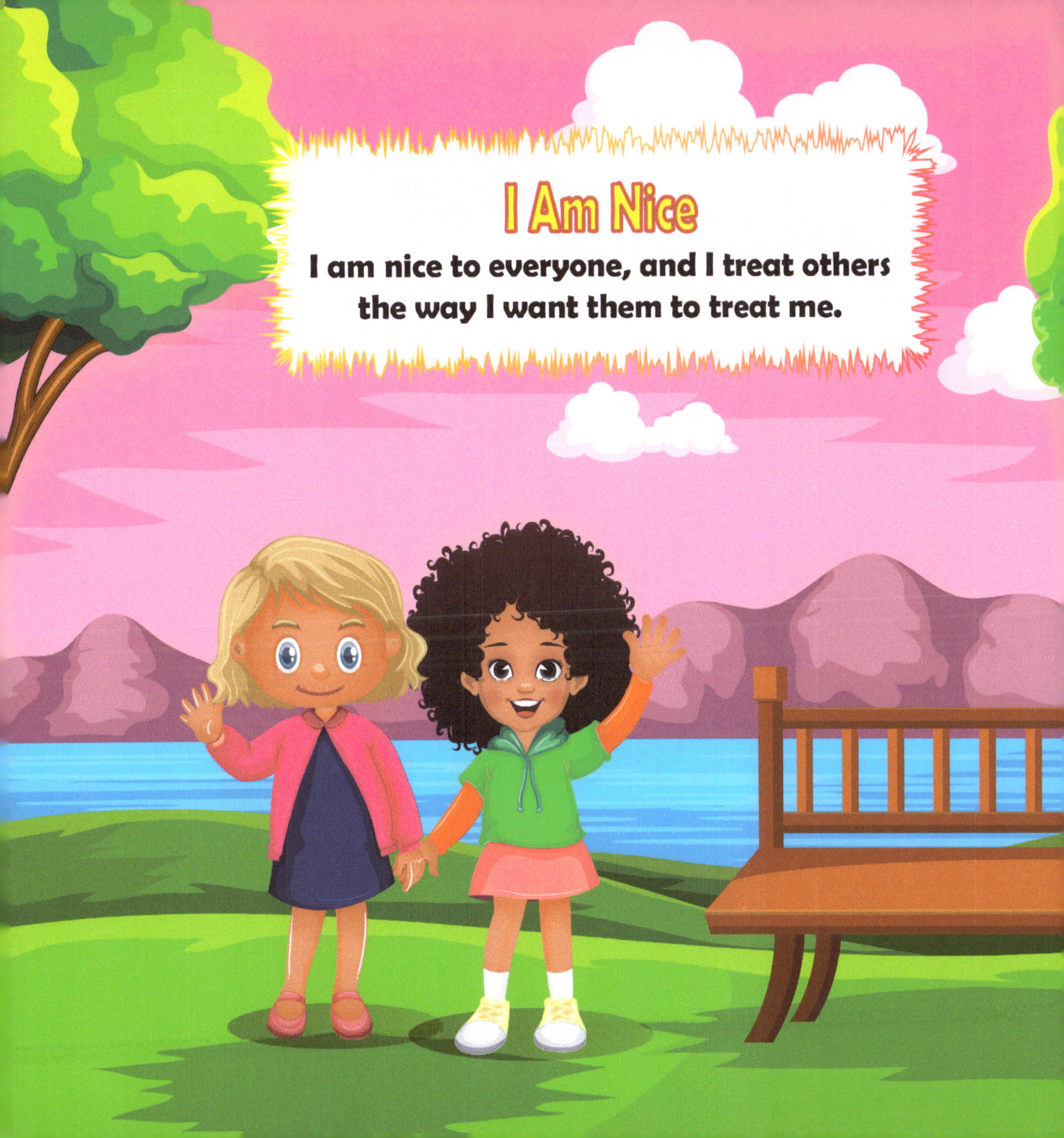

# I Am Nice

I am nice to everyone, and I treat others the way I want them to treat me.

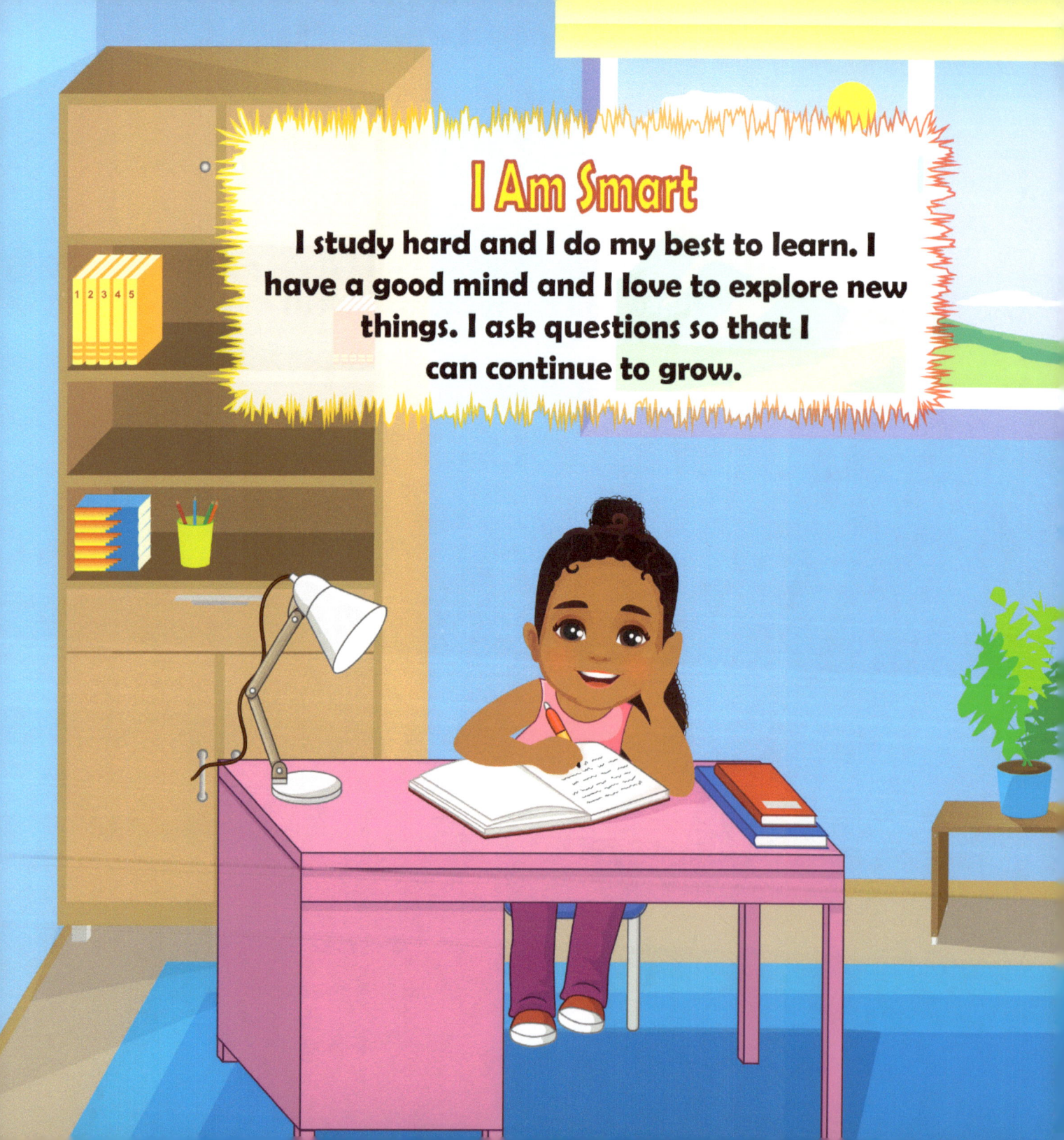

# I Am Smart

I study hard and I do my best to learn. I have a good mind and I love to explore new things. I ask questions so that I can continue to grow.

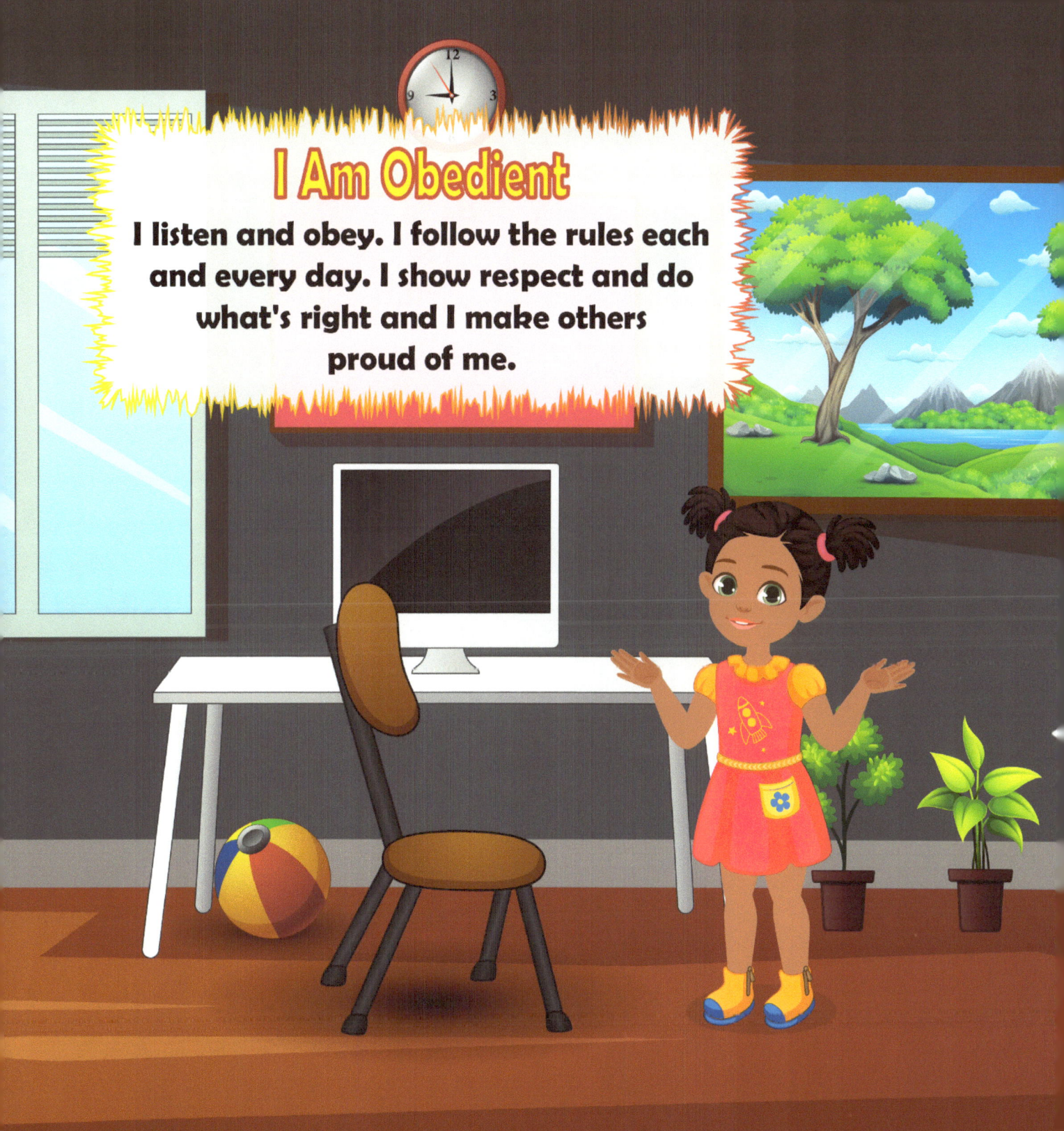

# I Am Obedient

I listen and obey. I follow the rules each and every day. I show respect and do what's right and I make others proud of me.

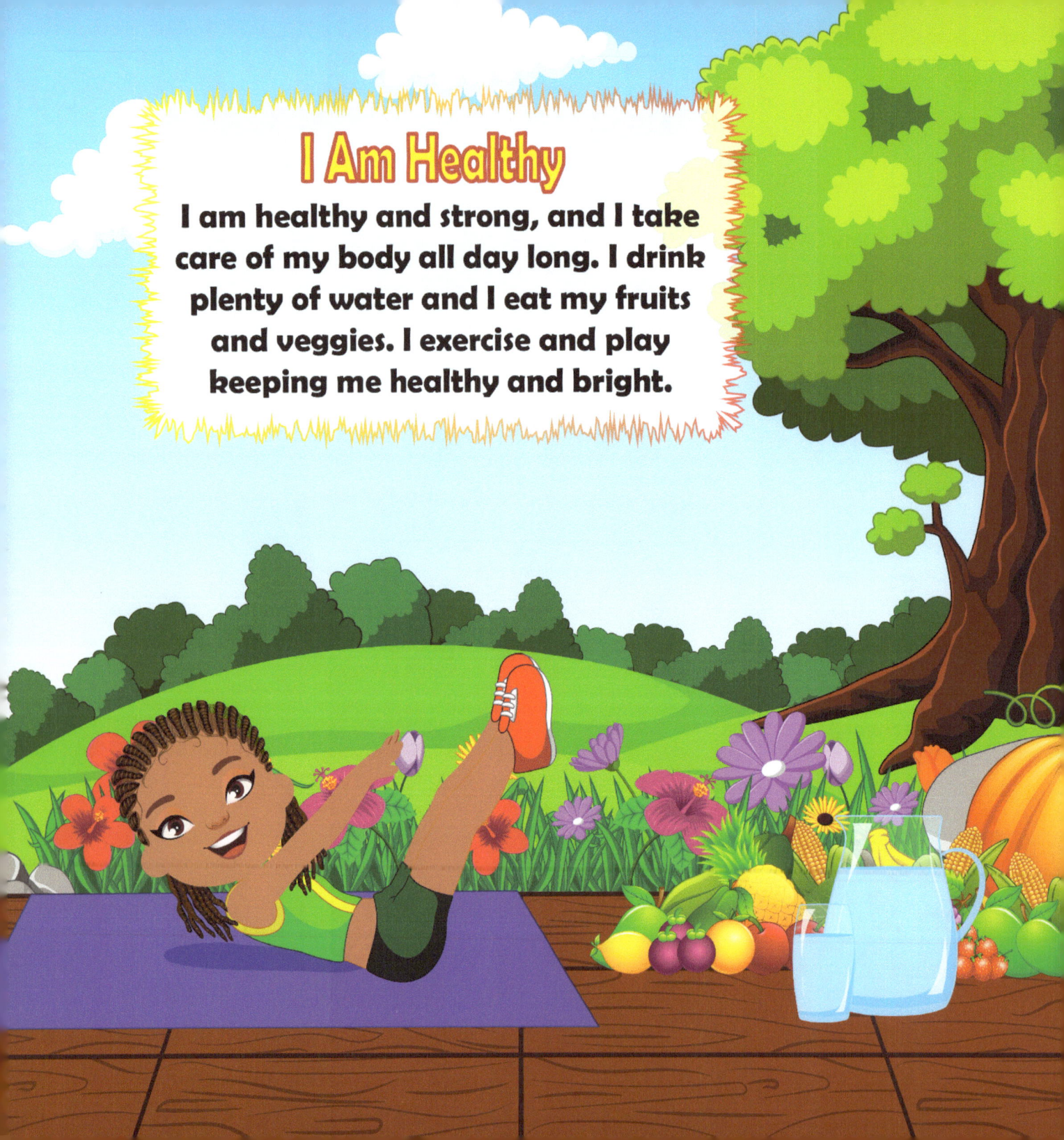

# I Am Healthy

I am healthy and strong, and I take care of my body all day long. I drink plenty of water and I eat my fruits and veggies. I exercise and play keeping me healthy and bright.

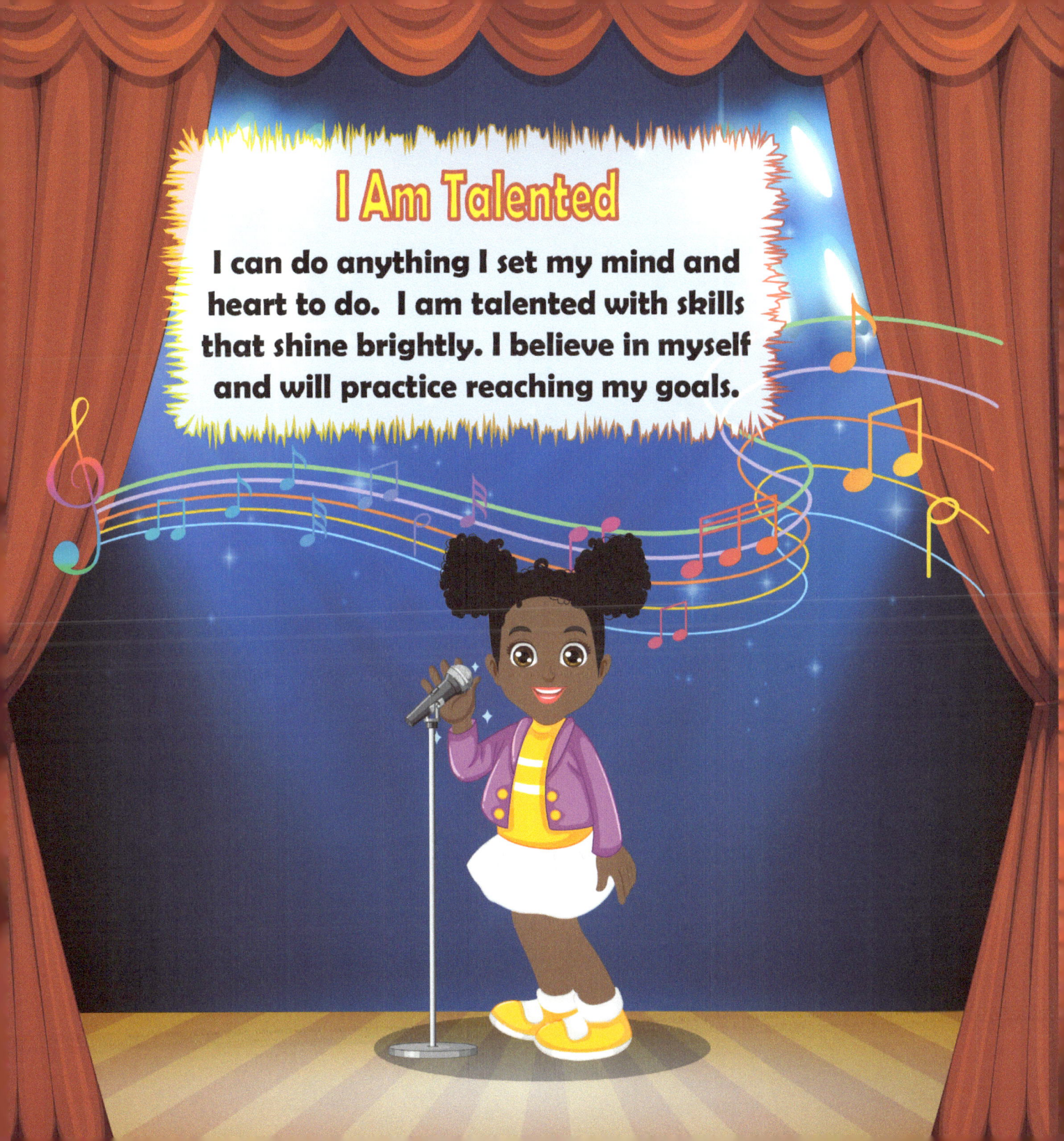

# I Am Talented

I can do anything I set my mind and heart to do. I am talented with skills that shine brightly. I believe in myself and will practice reaching my goals.

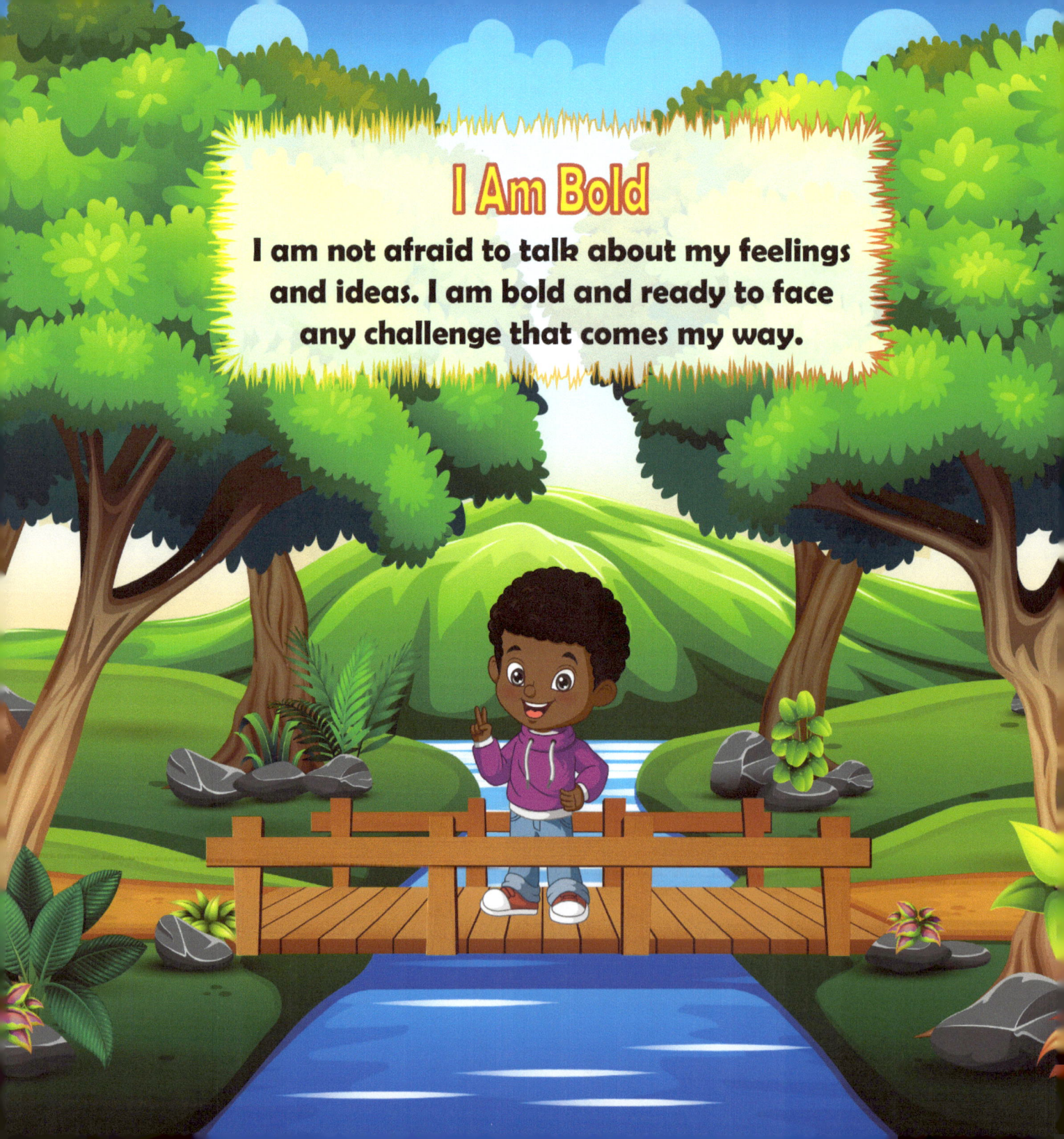

# I Am Bold

I am not afraid to talk about my feelings and ideas. I am bold and ready to face any challenge that comes my way.

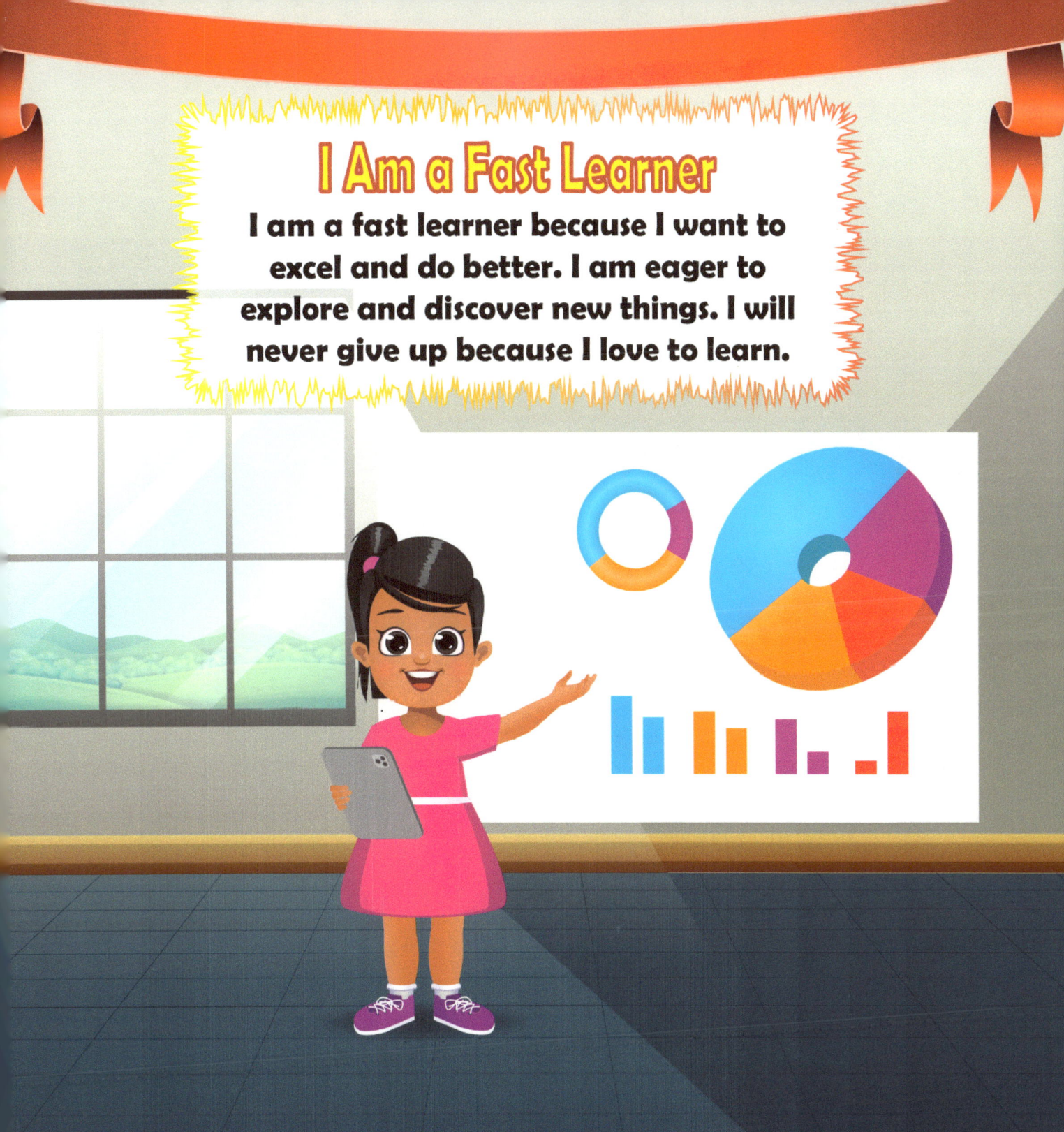

# I Am a Fast Learner

I am a fast learner because I want to excel and do better. I am eager to explore and discover new things. I will never give up because I love to learn.

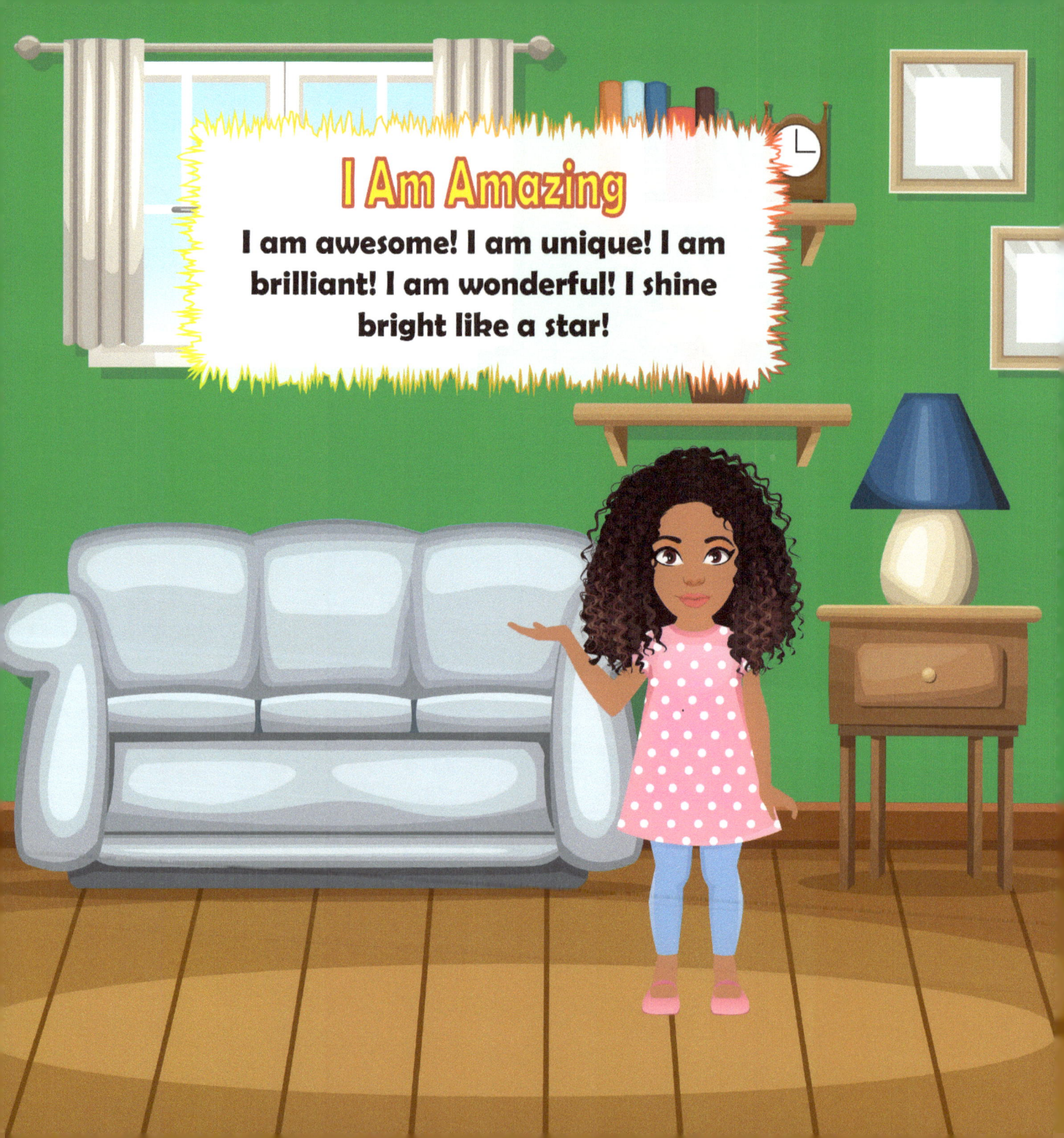

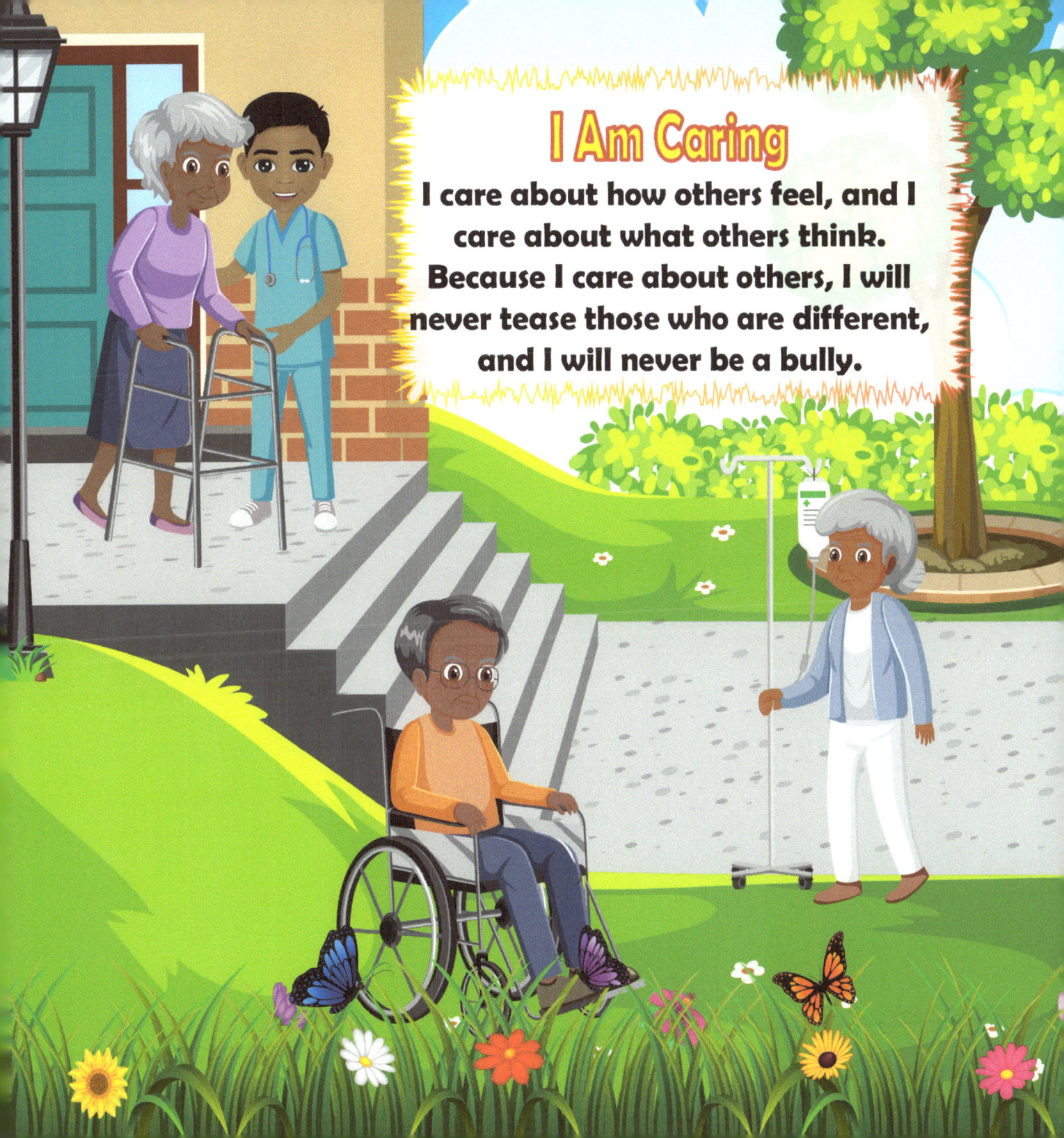

# I Am Caring

I care about how others feel, and I care about what others think. Because I care about others, I will never tease those who are different, and I will never be a bully.

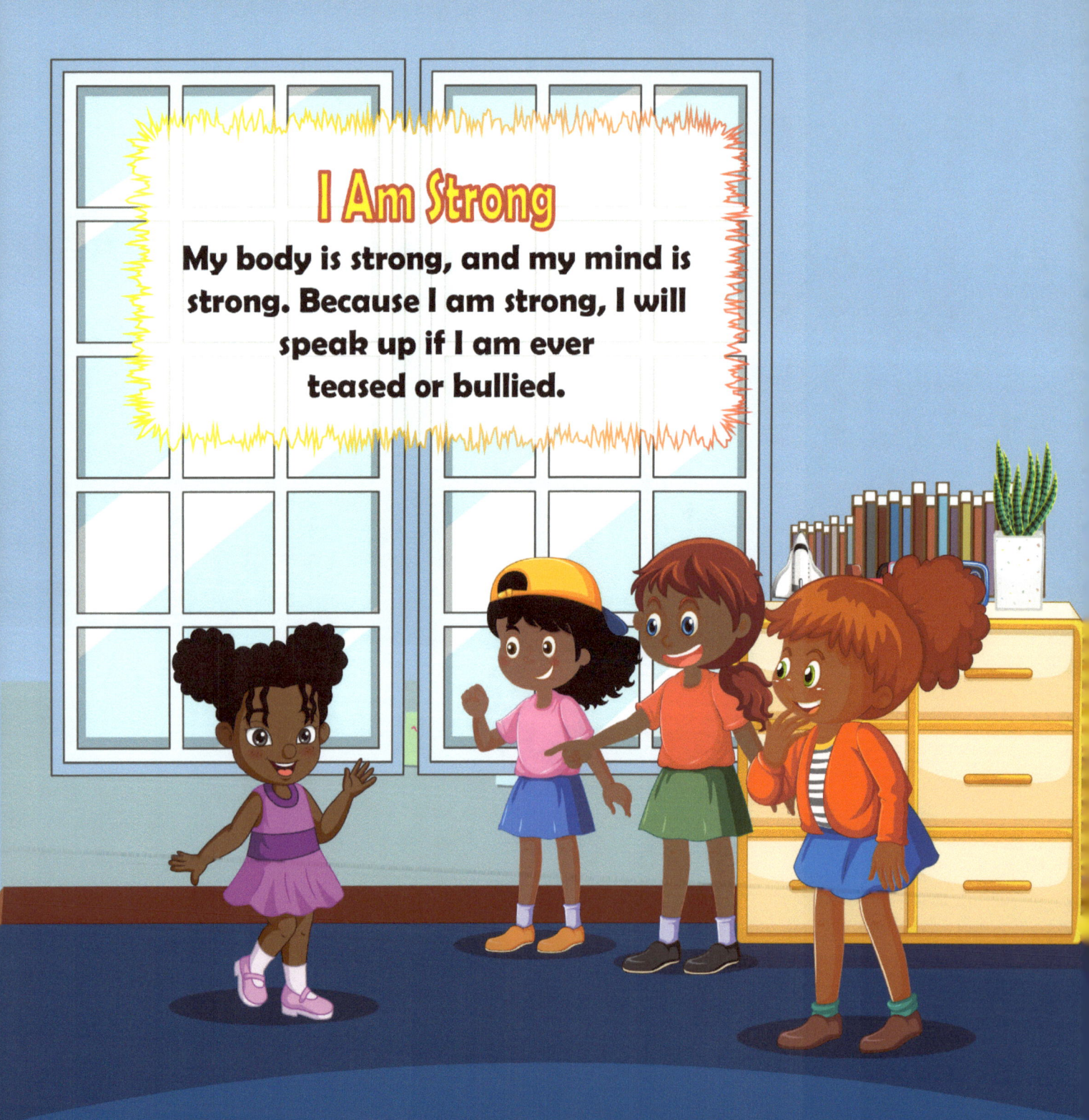

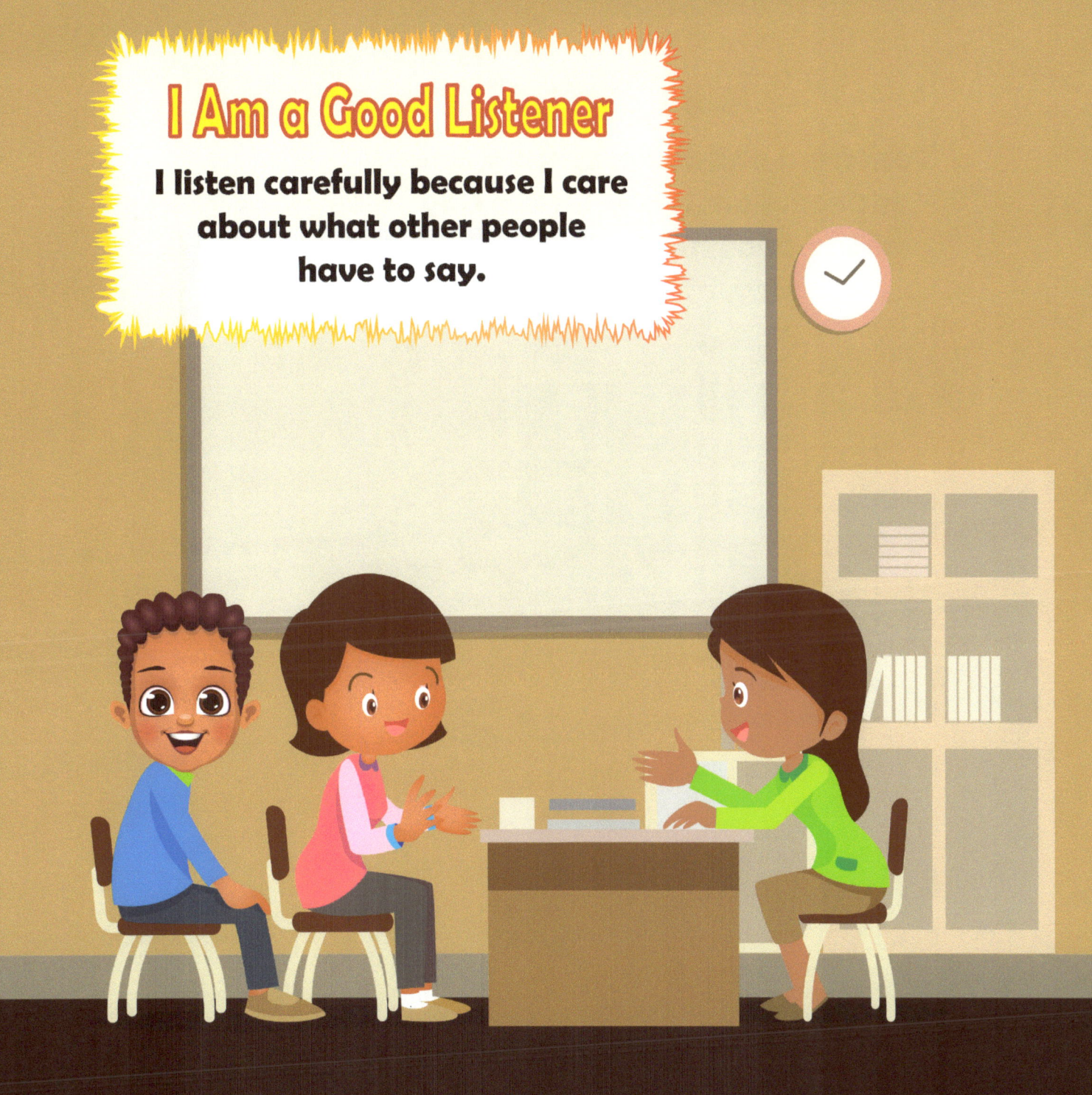

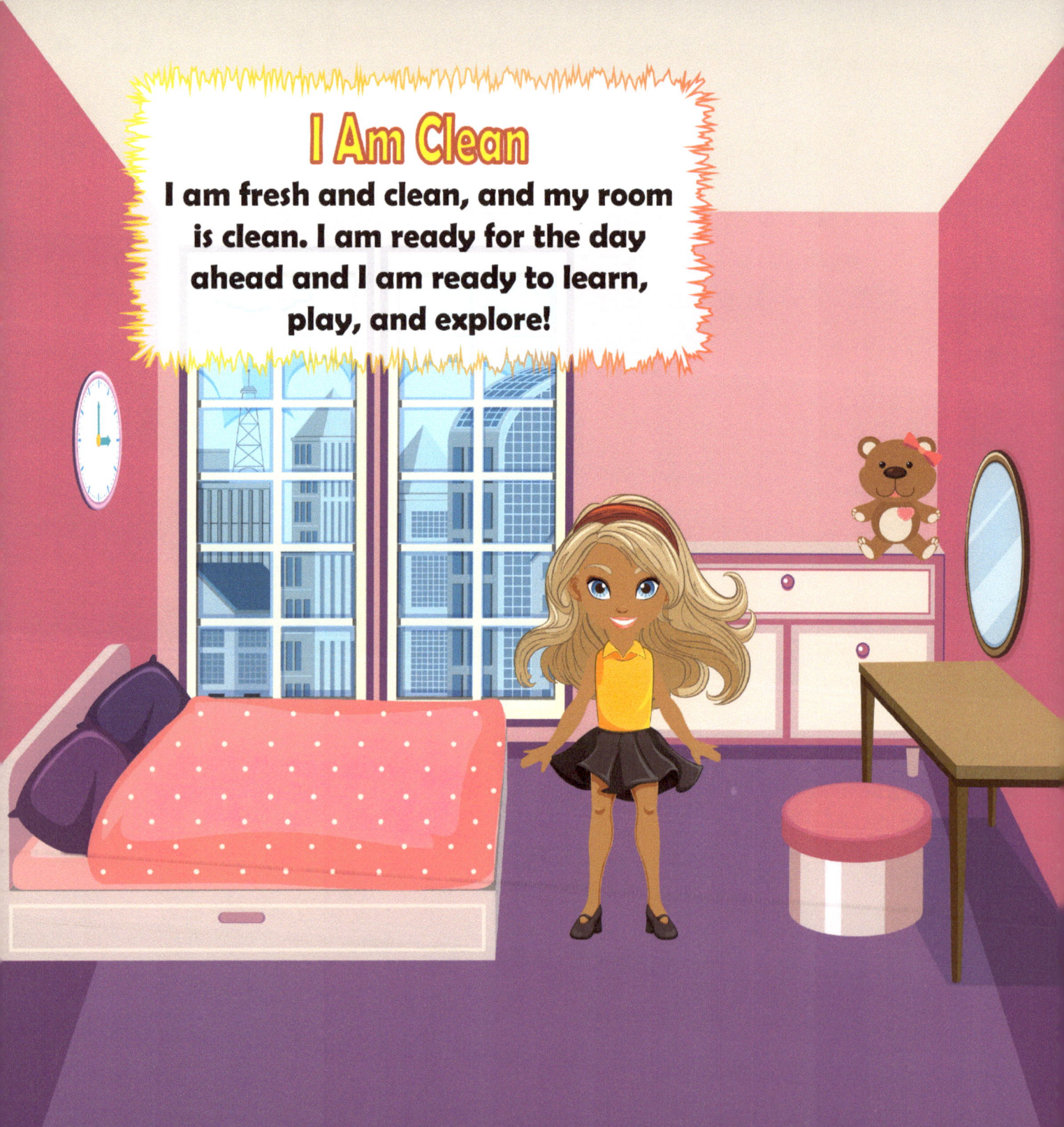

# I Am Clean

I am fresh and clean, and my room is clean. I am ready for the day ahead and I am ready to learn, play, and explore!

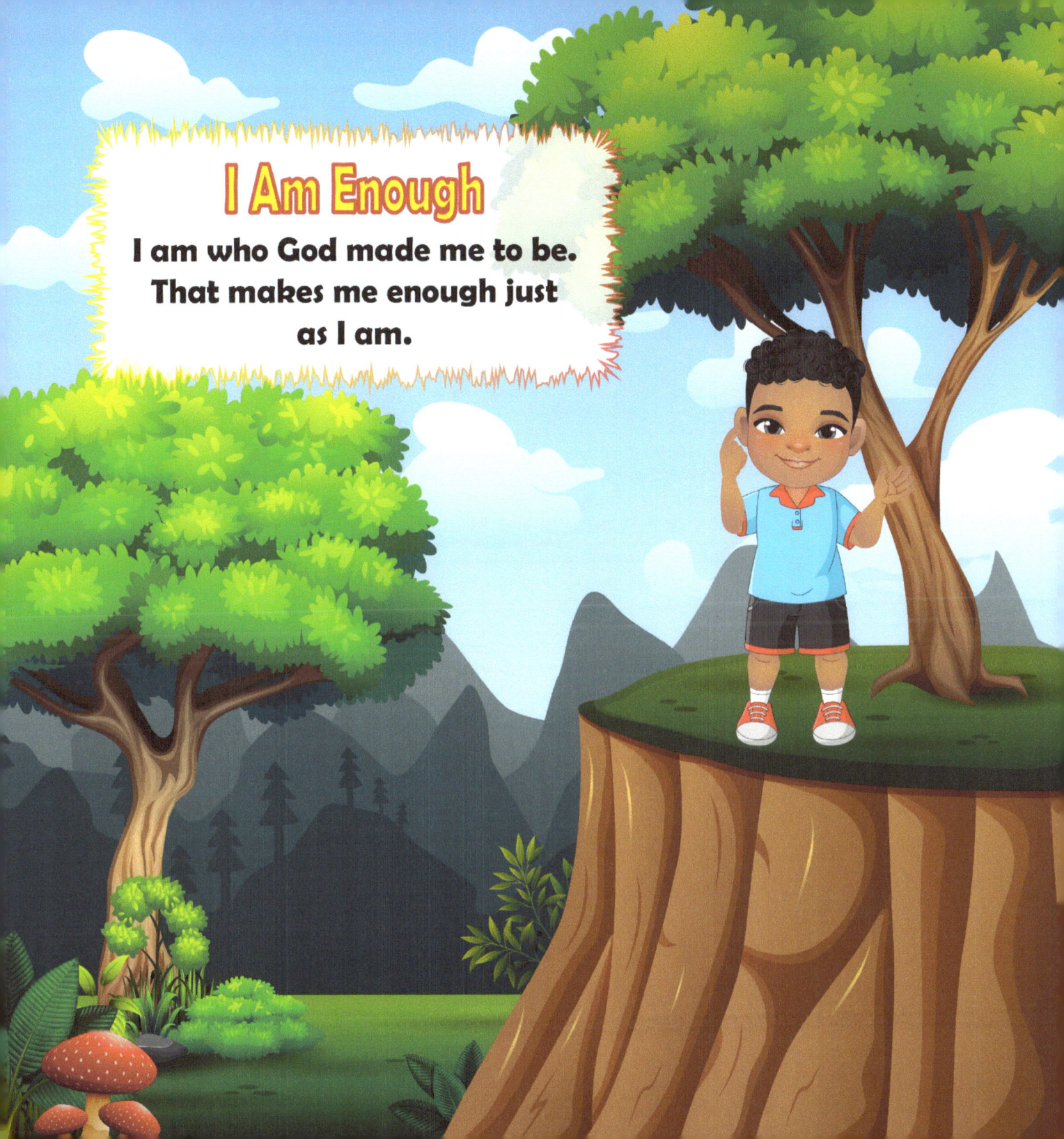

# I Am Enough

I am who God made me to be. That makes me enough just as I am.

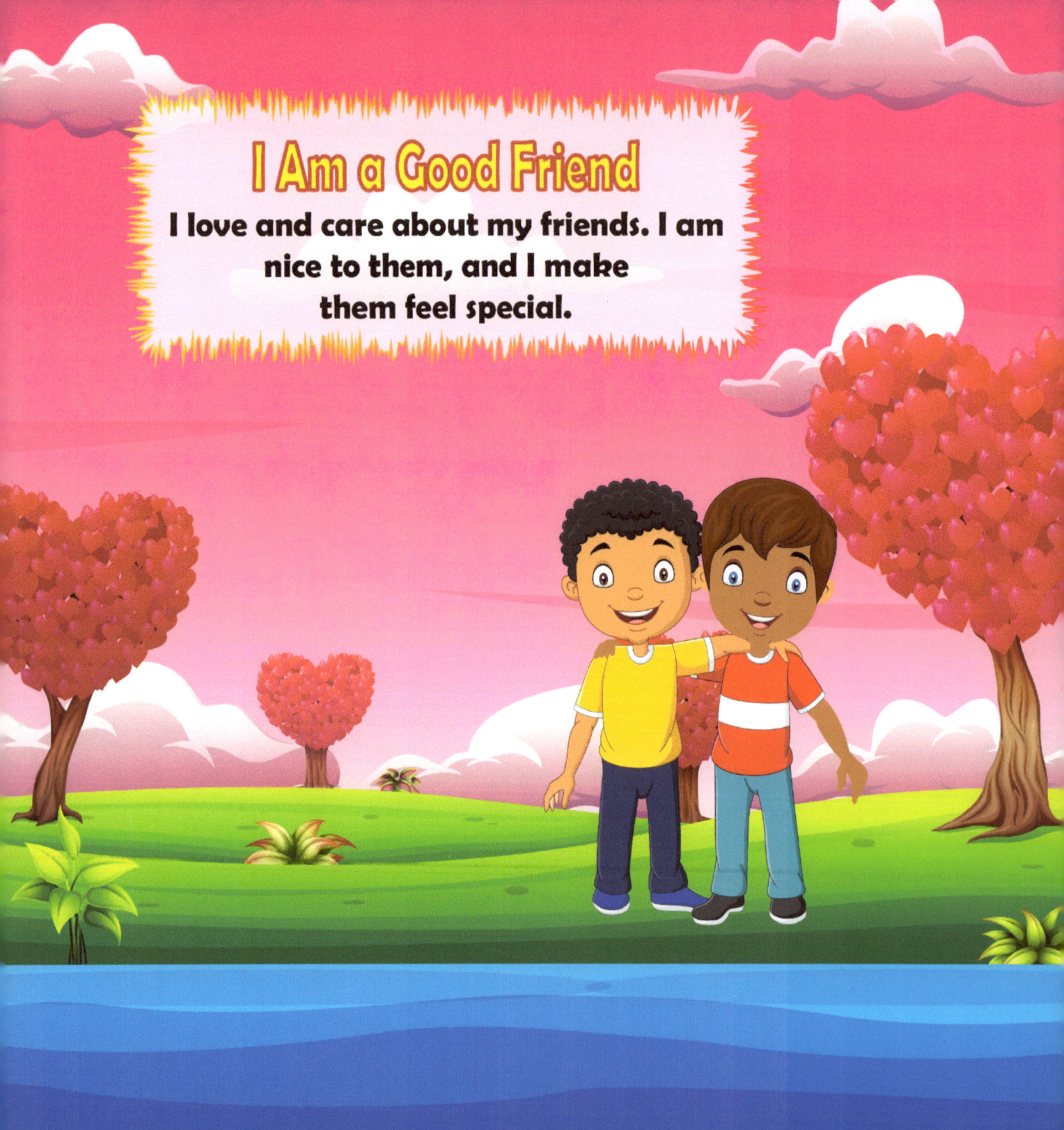

# I Am a Good Friend

I love and care about my friends. I am nice to them, and I make them feel special.

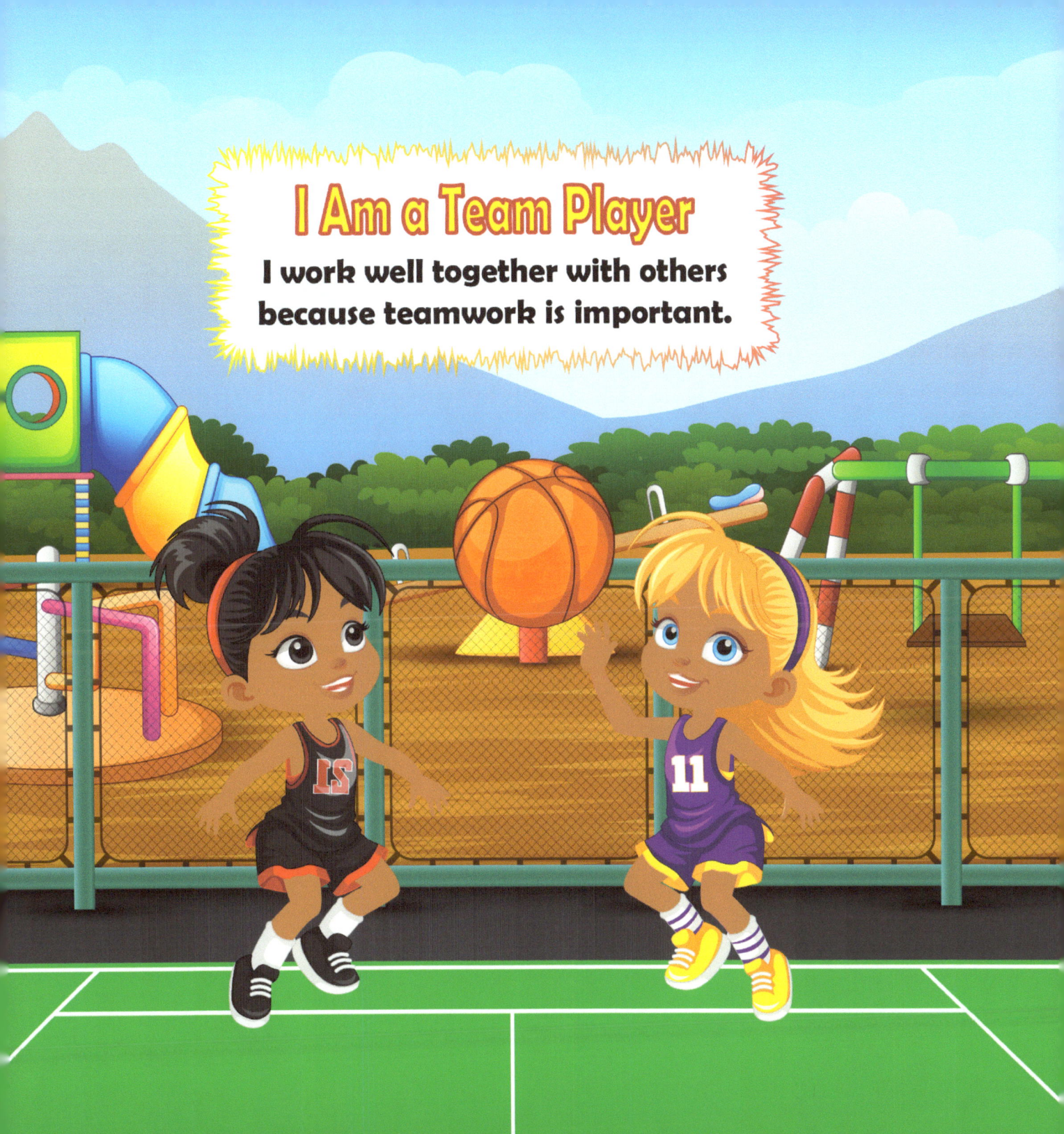

# I Am a Team Player

I work well together with others because teamwork is important.

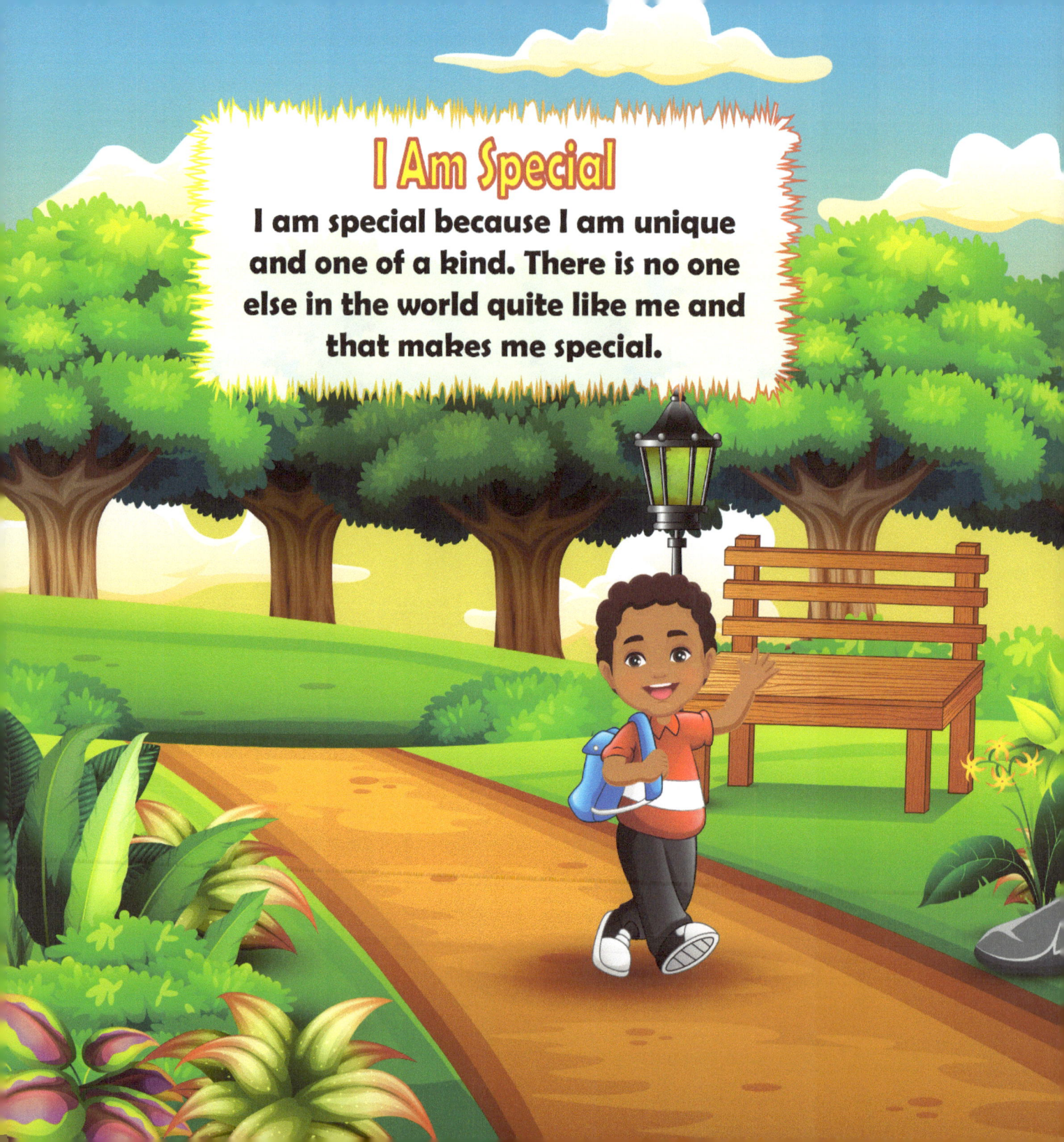

# I Am Special

I am special because I am unique and one of a kind. There is no one else in the world quite like me and that makes me special.

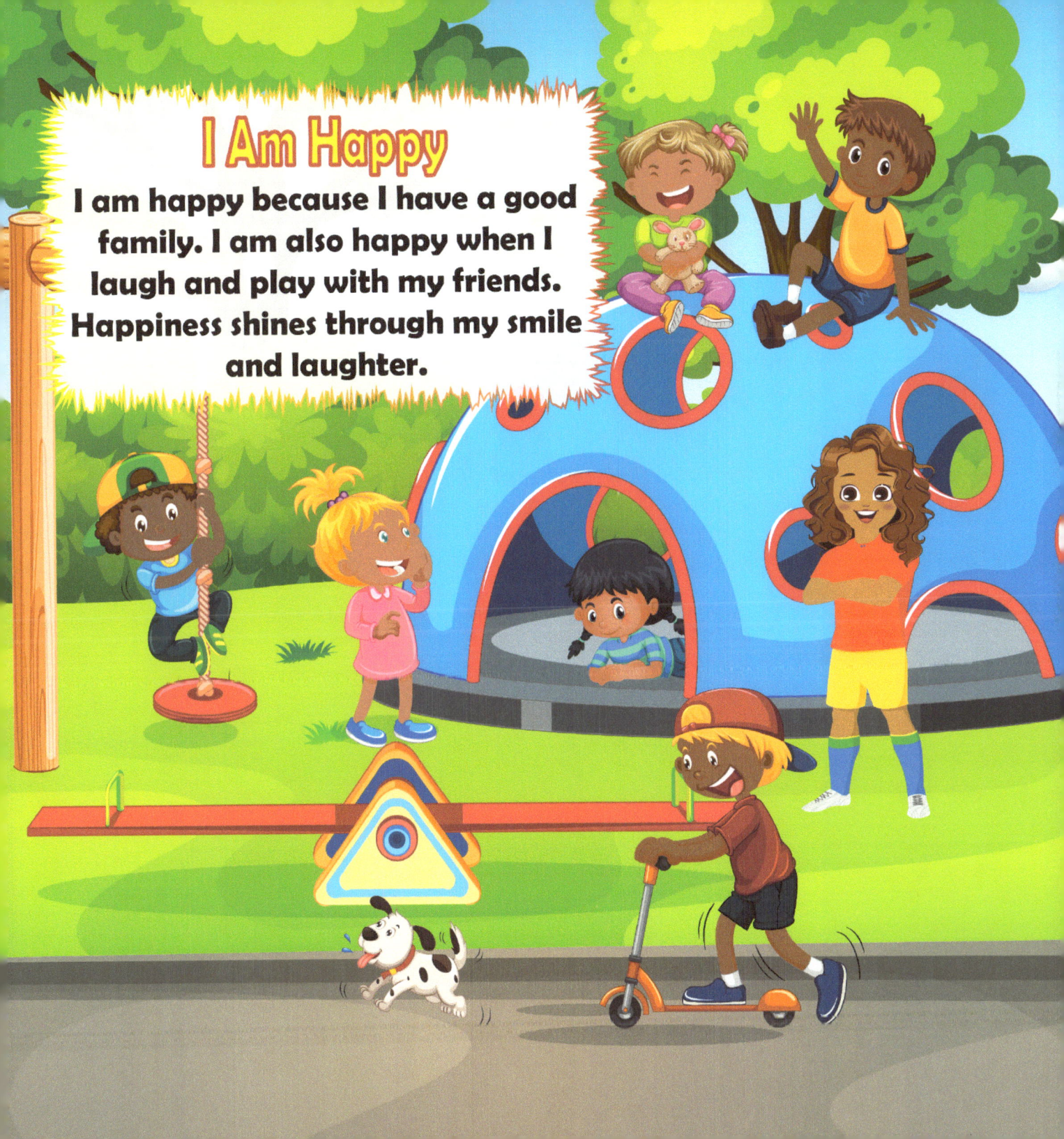

# I Am Happy

I am happy because I have a good family. I am also happy when I laugh and play with my friends. Happiness shines through my smile and laughter.

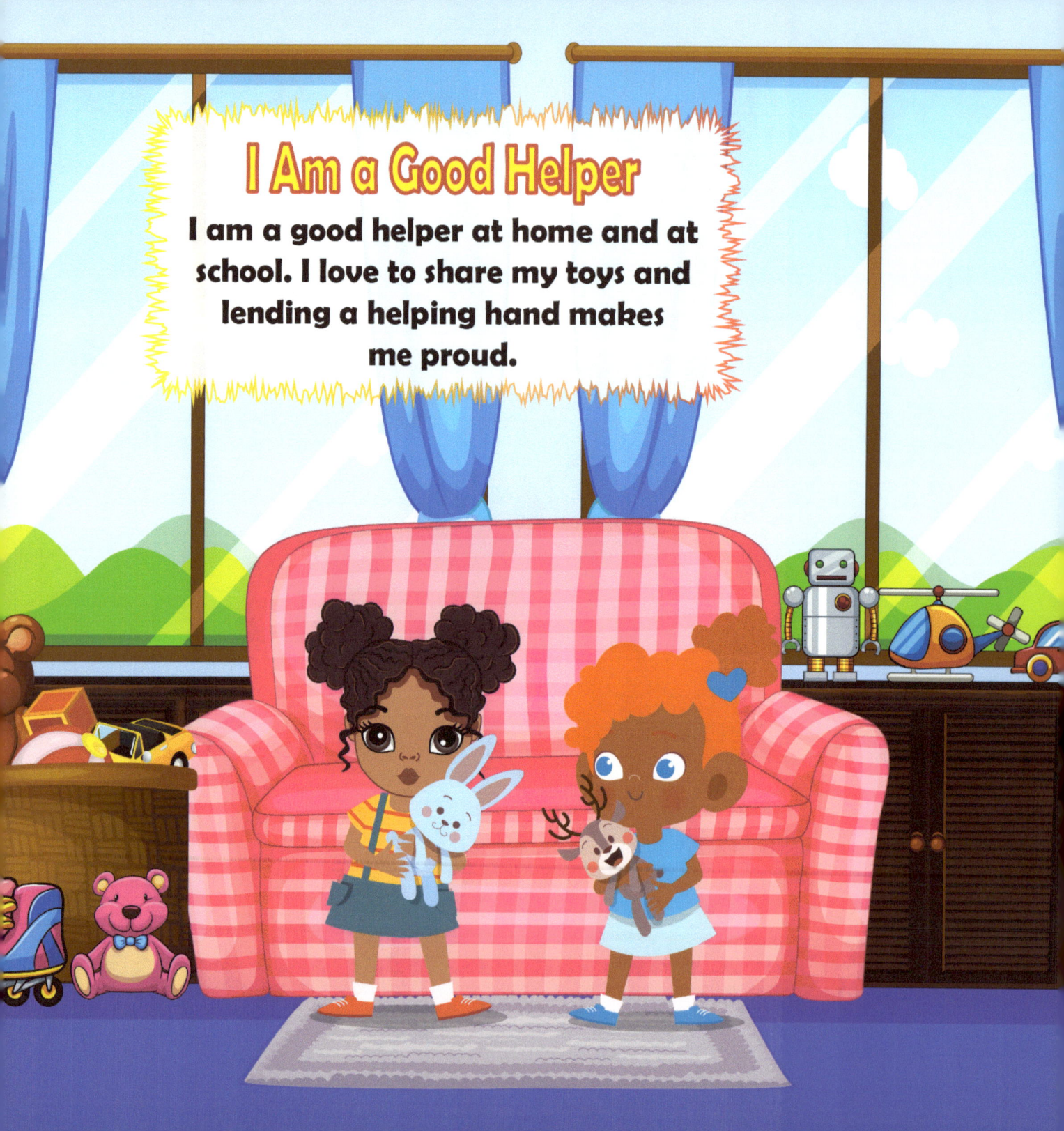

# I Am a Good Helper

I am a good helper at home and at school. I love to share my toys and lending a helping hand makes me proud.

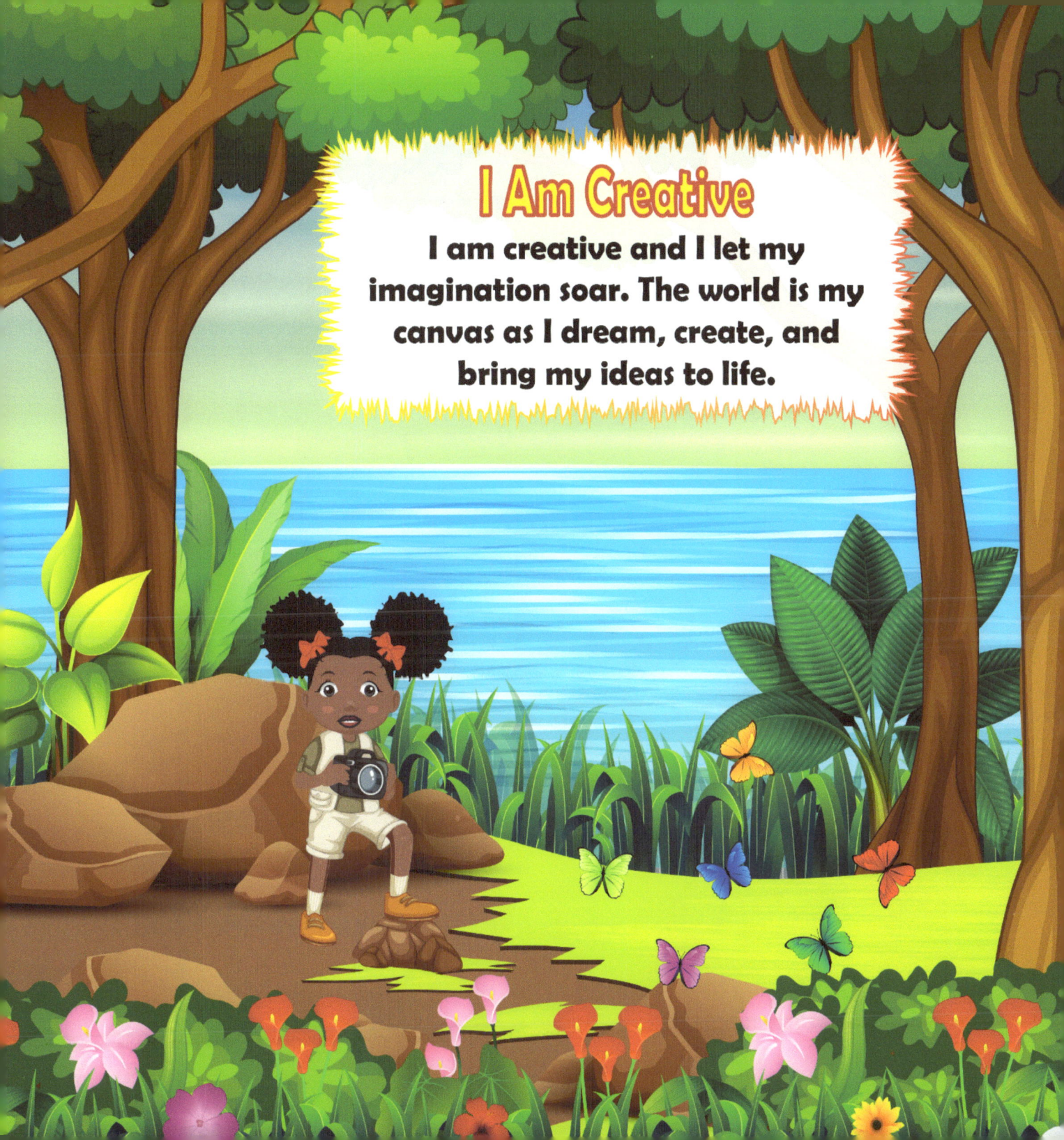

# I Am Creative

I am creative and I let my imagination soar. The world is my canvas as I dream, create, and bring my ideas to life.